# Story Elements
## A Bulletin Board in a Book!

# Sunflower
### education

*Exceptional Books for Teachers and Parents*

*Editorial*
Sunflower Education

*Design*
Cynthia Hannon Design

ISBN-13: 978-1-937166-16-8
ISBN-10: 1-937166-16-3
Copyright © 2013
Sunflower Education. All rights reserved. Printed in the U.S.A.

# Table of Contents

**To the Teacher**

**Activity Sheets**

Story Elements
Story Elements Graphic Organizer
Plot
Plot Graphic Organizer
Character
Character Graphic Organizer
Setting
Setting Graphic Organizer
Conflict
Conflict Graphic Organizer
Resolution
Resolution Graphic Organizer
Theme
Theme Graphic Organizer

**Posters**

Story Elements Title
Story Elements Definition
Plot, Definition, Questions
Character, Definition, Questions
Setting, Definition, Questions
Conflict, Definition, Questions
Resolution, Definition, Questions
Theme, Definition, Questions

© 2013 SunflowerEducation.net

# To the Teacher

*Story Elements: A Bulletin Board in a Book!* consists of two main parts: bulletin-board posters and student activity sheets. They are designed to be used together.

**There are 20 posters:**
- 1—Story Elements (title poster)
- 1—Story Elements Definition (subtitle poster)
- 6—Story Elements (plot, character, setting, conflict, resolution, theme)
- 6—Story Elements Definitions (plot, character, setting, conflict, resolution, theme)
- 6—Story Elements Questions (plot, character, setting, conflict, resolution, theme)

**There are 14 student activity sheets:**
- 1—on story elements in general
- 6—Story Elements (plot, character, setting, conflict, resolution, theme)
- 7—Graphic Organizers (story elements, plot, character, setting, conflict, resolution, theme)

### ❶ Post the Bulletin-Board Display
- Copy the posters or cut them out.
- Post the Story Elements (title poster) and Story Elements Definition (subtitle poster) posters together to form the top or central part of the display.
- Pair each Story Element poster with its corresponding Story Element Definition and Story Element Questions poster.

### ❷ Discuss Story Elements with Students
- Lead a discussion about story elements. Allow students time to peruse the posters. Ensure students understand each story element in isolation. Have them complete the story element activity sheets. All of the activity sheets can be completed using information from the posters. Consider having students complete the activity sheets either as assessment or with access to the bulletin board.
- Students can complete the activity sheets individually or with partners.
- Next, lead students through a familiar story (e.g., Cinderella, or another one you are reading together) and guide them in identifying each of the story's elements.

### ❸ Guide Students in Applying What They Learn
- Help students complete the story element graphic organizers for stories they read on their own.

Have fun sharing great stories with your students!

---

## Worksheet Answers

**Story Elements**
1. Part
2. Six
3. Verify correct matches.

**Plot**
1. The plot is what happens in the story.
2. What are the events in the story? In what order do the events happen?
3. Answer should demonstrate an understanding of plot.
4. Reward earnest answers.

**Character**
1. The characters are the people that take part in the plot. Characters can also be animals or things.
2. Who are the characters in the story? Who are the major characters? Who are the minor characters? What traits does each character have?
3. Answer should demonstrate an understanding of character.
4. Reward earnest answers.

**Setting**
1. The setting is where and when the story takes place.
2. Where does the story take place? When does the story take place?
3. Answer should demonstrate an understanding of setting.
4. Reward earnest answers.

**Conflict**
1. The conflict is a problem that the characters in the story face. Conflict occurs when characters disagree with each other.
2. What problem or problems do the characters face? What characters disagree with each other?
3. Answer should demonstrate an understanding of conflict.
4. Reward earnest answers.

**Resolution**
1. The resolution is the solution to the conflict in the story.
2. How is the problem solved? How is the conflict resolved?
3. Answer should demonstrate an understanding of resolution.
4. Reward earnest answers.

**Theme**
1. The theme is the message or lesson of a story. There can be one main theme or many themes.
2. What is the message or lesson of the story? What is another message or lesson of the story?
3. Answer should demonstrate an understanding of theme.
4. Reward earnest answers.

Name _____  Class _____  Date _____

# Story Elements

**1** What does the word *element* mean?

_____

**2** How many story elements are there?

_____

**3** Match each story element to the correct definition by drawing a line.

**plot**              the people that take part in the plot

**character**         this occurs when characters disagree with each other

**setting**           the solution to the conflict in the story

**conflict**          the message or lesson of a story

**resolution**        what happens in the story

**theme**             where and when the story takes place

Name _____  Class _____  Date _____

# Story Elements

| | |
|---|---|
| **Plot** | **Character** |
| **Setting** | **Conflict** |
| **Resolution** | **Theme** |

© 2013 SunflowerEducation.net

Name _____  Class _____  Date _____

# Plot

**1** Write a definition of the word *plot*.

_____
_____
_____

**2** What questions does the plot of a story answer?

_____
_____
_____

**3** Why is it important for a story to have a plot?

_____
_____
_____

**4** Tell about the plot of a story you like.

_____
_____
_____
_____

Name _____ Class _____ Date _____

# Plot

⑤ Resolution (Denouement)

④ Falling Action

③ Climax

② Rising Action

① Introduction (Exposition)

Name _____ Class _____ Date _____

# Character

**1** Write a definition of the word *character*.

_____
_____

**2** What questions do the characters of a story answer?

_____
_____
_____
_____

**3** Why is it important for a story to have characters?

_____
_____

**4** Tell about a character in a story you like.

_____
_____
_____

Name _____ Class _____ Date _____

# Character

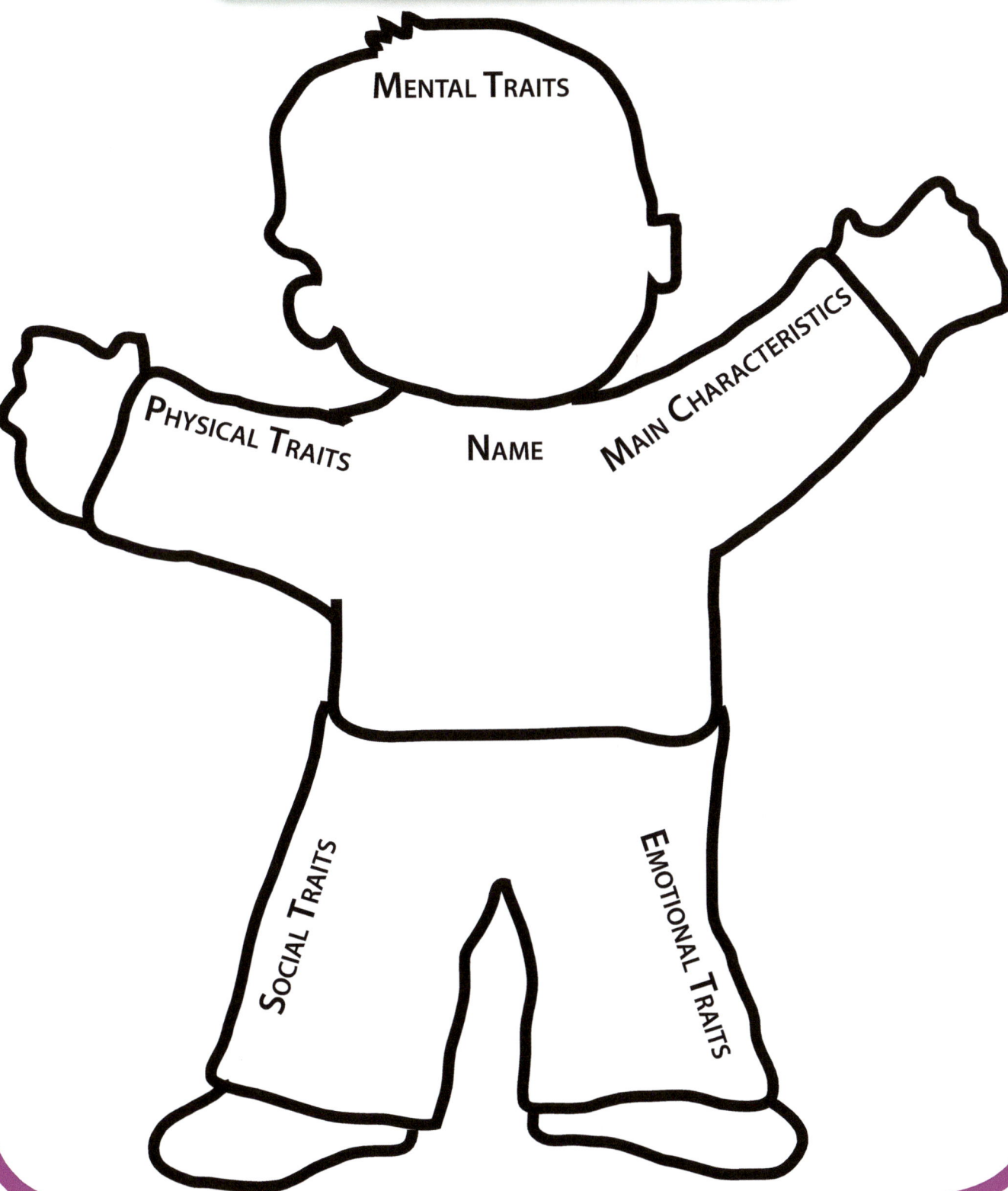

Name _____ Class _____ Date _____

# Setting

**1** Write a definition of the word *setting*.

_____
_____
_____

**2** What questions does the setting of a story answer?

_____
_____

**3** Why is it important for a story to have a setting?

_____
_____

**4** Tell about the setting of a story you like.

_____
_____
_____
_____

© 2013 SunflowerEducation.net

Name _____ Class _____ Date _____

# Setting

**P**LACE

_____

**S**ETTING

_____

**T**IME

Name _____ Class _____ Date _____

# Conflict

**1** Write a definition of the word *conflict*.

_____
_____
_____

**2** What questions does the conflict of a story answer?

_____
_____

**3** Why is it important for a story to have conflict?

_____
_____

**4** Tell about the conflict in a story you like.

_____
_____
_____
_____

Name _____ Class _____ Date _____

# Conflict

☐ v. ☐

☐ v. ☐

☐ v. ☐

Name _____ Class _____ Date _____

# Resolution

**1** Write a definition of the word *resolution*.

_____

_____

_____


**2** What questions does the resolution of a story answer?

_____

_____


**3** Why is it important for a story to have a resolution?

_____

_____


**4** Tell about the resolution of a story you like.

_____

_____

_____

_____

Name _____ Class _____ Date _____

# Resolution

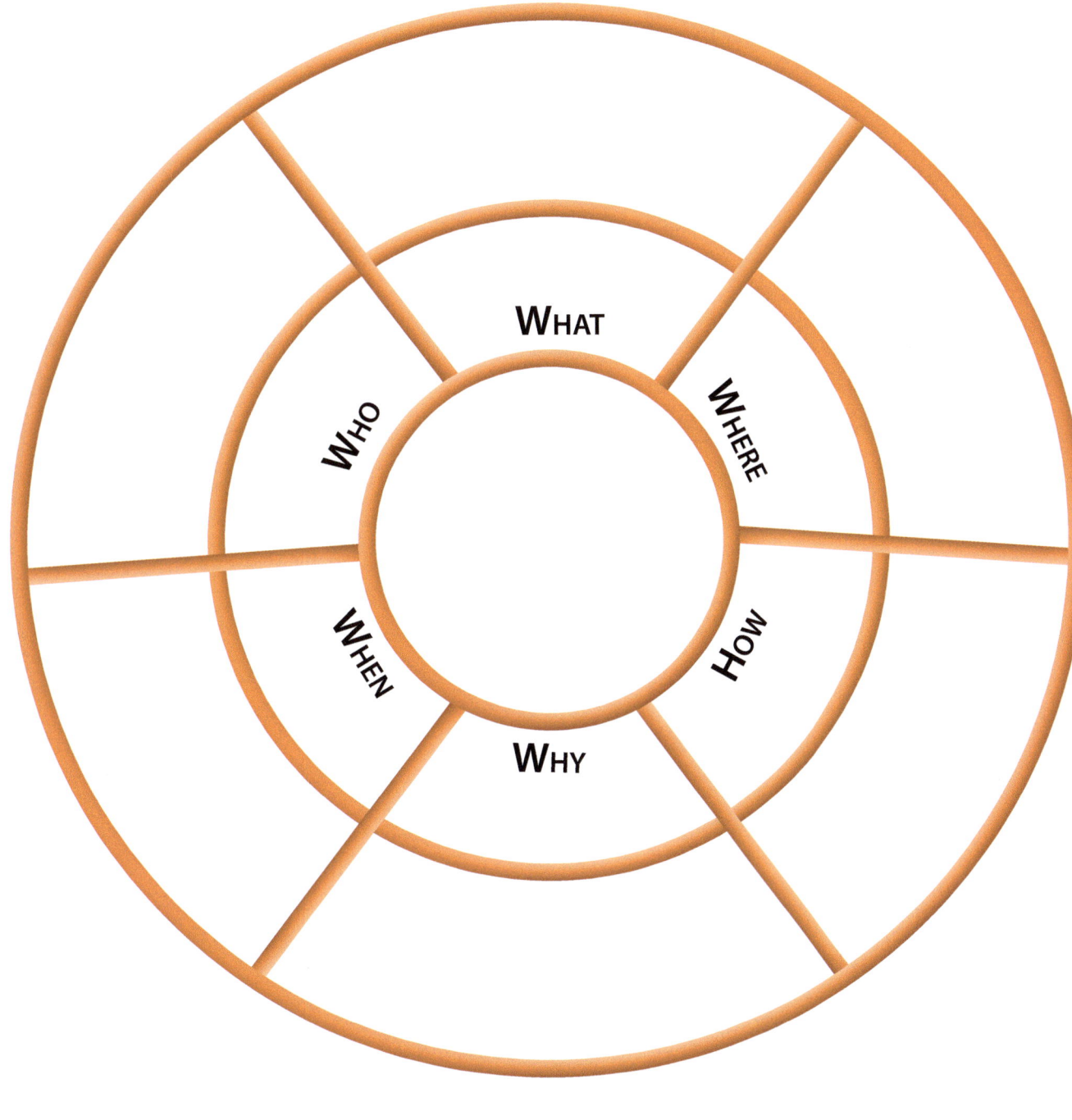

Name _____ Class _____ Date _____

# Theme

**1** Write a definition of the word *theme*.

_____

_____

_____

**2** What questions does the theme of a story answer?

_____

_____

**3** Why is it important for a story to have a theme?

_____

_____

**4** Tell about the theme of a story you like.

_____

_____

_____

_____

© 2013 SunflowerEducation.net

Name _____ Class _____ Date _____

# Theme

Reasons

Theme

# Story Elements

**Story Elements** are the parts of a story. The word *elements* means "parts." There are six story elements:

① **Plot**

② **Character**

③ **Setting**

④ **Conflict**

⑤ **Resolution**

⑥ **Theme**

# Plot

**The plot is what happens in the story.**

# Plot Questions

- What are the events in the story?
- In what order do the events happen?

# Character

The **characters** are the people that take part in the plot. Characters can also be animals or things.

# Character Questions

- **Who are the characters in the story?**
- **Who are the *major* characters?**
- **Who are the *minor* characters?**
- **What *traits* does each character have?**

# Setting

The **setting** is *where* and *when* the story takes place.

# Setting Questions

- **Where does the story take place?**
- **When does the story take place?**

# Conflict

The **conflict** is a problem that the characters in the story face. Conflict occurs when characters disagree with each other.

# Conflict Questions

- What problem or problems do the characters face?
- What characters disagree with each other?

# Resolution

The **resolution** is the solution to the conflict in the story.

# Resolution Questions

- **How is the problem solved?**
- **How is the conflict resolved?**

# Theme

The **theme** is the message or lesson of a story. There can be one main theme or many themes.

# Theme Questions

- **What is the message or lesson of the story?**

- **What is another message or lesson of the story?**

www.ingramcontent.com/pod-product-compliance
Lightning Source LLC
Chambersburg PA
CBHW041534040426
42446CB00002B/79